# Oceans and Seas

# Pacific Ocean

John F. Prevost
ABDO Publishing Company

# visit us at
# www.abdopub.com

Published by ABDO Publishing Company, 4940 Viking Drive, Edina, Minnesota 55435.
Copyright © 2003 by Abdo Consulting Group, Inc. International copyrights reserved in
all countries. No part of this book may be reproduced in any form without written
permission from the publisher.

Printed in the United States.

Photo Credits: Corbis

Contributing Editors: Kate A. Conley, Kristin Van Cleaf, Kristianne E. Vieregger
Art Direction & Maps: Neil Klinepier

## Library of Congress Cataloging-in-Publication Data

Prevost, John F.
    Pacific Ocean / John F. Prevost.
      p. cm. -- (Oceans and seas)
    Includes bibliographical references and index.
    Summary: Surveys the origin, geological borders, climate, water, plant and animal
life, and economic and ecological aspects of the Pacific Ocean.
    ISBN 1-57765-093-X
    1. Pacific Ocean--Juvenile literature. [1. Pacific Ocean.] I. Title. II. Series: Prevost,
  John F. Oceans and seas.
GC771.P717 1999
551.46'5--dc21
                                                      98-12069
                                                      CIP
                                                       AC

# Contents

# The Pacific Ocean

The Pacific Ocean is the largest ocean in the world. This massive body of water covers almost one-third of the globe! Its waters separate North and South America from Asia and Australia.

The **equator** divides the Pacific Ocean into two parts. North of the equator lies the North Pacific Ocean. South of the equator lies the South Pacific Ocean. Both parts include islands and **seas**.

The Pacific Ocean has not always looked as it does today. About 200 million years ago, Earth had only one large ocean. It was called Panthalassa. It surrounded Earth's only continent, Pangaea.

Over time, Pangaea broke into pieces. These pieces became today's seven continents. The continents slowly drifted across Earth, dividing Panthalassa into new oceans. The Pacific is the oldest of these oceans.

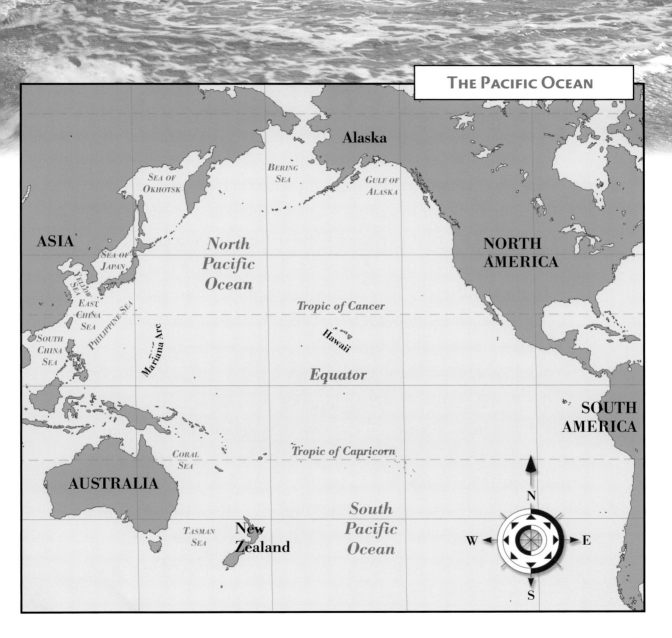

Alaska

SEA OF
OKHOTSK

BERING
SEA

GULF OF
ALASKA

ASIA

SEA OF
JAPAN

North
Pacific
Ocean

NORTH
AMERICA

YELLOW
SEA

EAST
CHINA
SEA

PHILIPPINE SEA

Tropic of Cancer

SOUTH
CHINA
SEA

Mariana Arc

Hawaii

Equator

SOUTH
AMERICA

CORAL
SEA

Tropic of Capricorn

AUSTRALIA

TASMAN
SEA

New
Zealand

South
Pacific
Ocean

N

W        E

S

# The Pacific Plate

Scientists believe Earth's surface is divided into sections called plates. Earth has about 12 large plates and several smaller ones. Earth's continents and oceans sit on top of these plates. Most of the Pacific Ocean sits on the Pacific Plate.

Hot, **molten** rock deep within Earth moves the plates. The Pacific Plate moves about 4 to 5 inches (10 to 13 cm) each year. This causes major activity along the plate boundaries.

When two plates slide against each other, earthquakes occur. In the Pacific, underwater earthquakes can cause giant waves called tsunamis. A tsunami can cross the entire Pacific Ocean in less than 24 hours! Once on shore, a tsunami can injure people and damage buildings in its path.

In areas where one plate slides under another, volcanoes are common. The Pacific Ocean has 336 active volcanoes. Most of these volcanoes are along the Pacific Plate's border. They form a chain called the Ring of Fire.

6

When two plates pull apart, **molten** rock rises from deep within Earth to fill the gap. This creates new ocean floor. Volcanoes are also common in these areas. Explorer Ridge in the northeast Pacific is an example of this.

*A volcano in the Pacific erupts.*

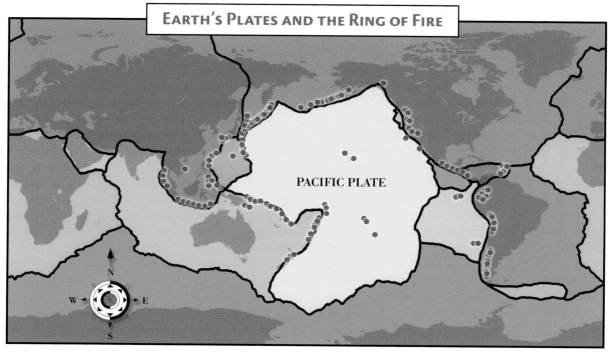

### EARTH'S PLATES AND THE RING OF FIRE

PACIFIC PLATE

# The Ocean Floor

The Pacific Ocean's floor has many different features. They formed over millions of years as Earth's plates moved. Today, the Pacific Ocean's floor continues to change.

One of the Pacific's best-known features is the Mariana Trench. It contains Earth's deepest point, Challenger Deep. Challenger Deep is 36,198 feet (11,033 m) below **sea level**.

The Pacific Ocean also has underwater volcanoes called seamounts. Some seamounts reach above the water's surface. This forms islands, such as the Mariana Arc.

Along North and South America, the Pacific Ocean's floor is marked by fracture zones. Fracture zones are long cracks in the ocean floor. They form when Earth's plates move.

Ridges also cover parts of the Pacific Ocean's floor. The Macquarie Ridge separates the Pacific and Indian Oceans. A ridge called the East Pacific Rise dominates the ocean floor in the eastern Pacific.

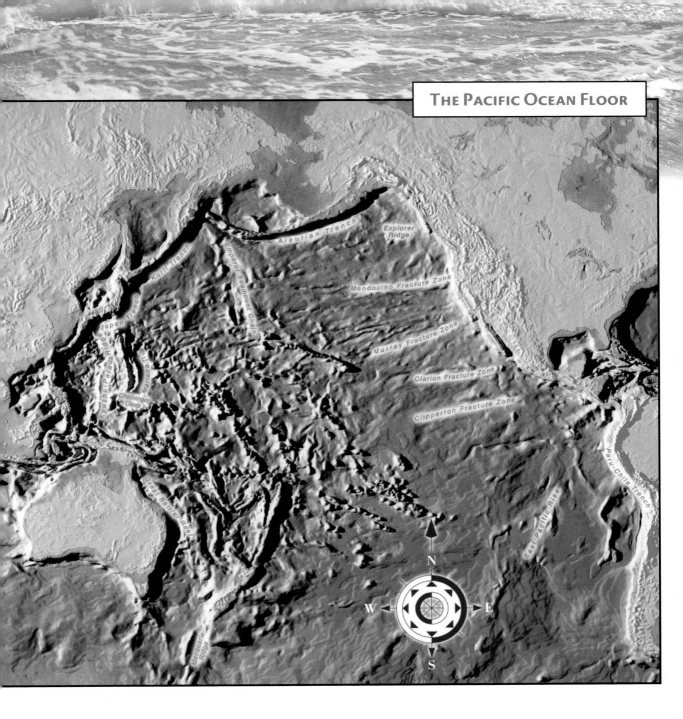

Explorer Ridge

Aleutian Trench

Emperor Seamount Chain

Kuril Trench

Japan Trench

Mendocino Fracture Zone

Murray Fracture Zone

Clarion Fracture Zone

Clipperton Fracture Zone

Kyushu Palau Ridge

Izu Bonin Trench

Challenger Deep

Mariana Trench

Great Barrier Reef

Peru-Chile Trench

East Pacific Rise

Macquarie Ridge

N
W    E
S

# Pacific Waters

The Pacific Ocean's water comes from rain, ice, and rivers. The Pacific's water continually moves from Earth, into the atmosphere, and back to Earth again. This process is called the hydrologic cycle.

The Pacific Ocean's water contains **dissolved** salt and other minerals. Waters near the **tropics of Cancer and Capricorn** are the saltiest in the Pacific. Areas where freshwater rivers empty into the Pacific are less salty.

Temperature greatly affects the Pacific's water. Cold water is much **denser** than warm water. For this reason, cold water sinks to the deeper parts of the Pacific. The warmer water rises to the surface.

Currents are streams of water flowing through the ocean. Currents in the Pacific follow two main patterns. In the North Pacific, currents move clockwise. In the South Pacific, they move counterclockwise.

Tides raise and lower the Pacific's water level. The moon causes tides. Its gravity pulls ocean water toward the moon. High tides occur at places on Earth that are nearest and farthest from the moon. Low tides occur in between.

## THE HYDROLOGIC CYCLE

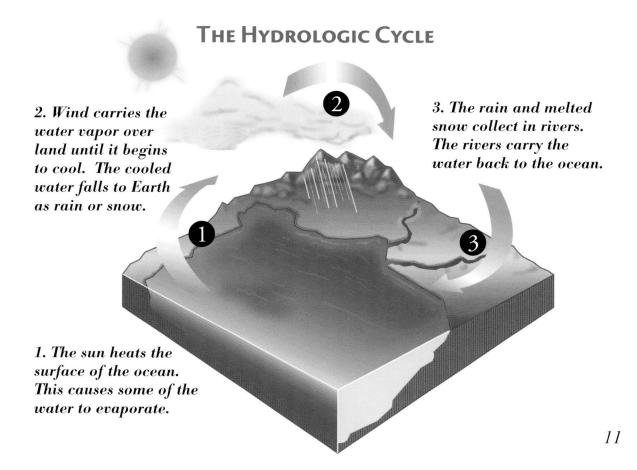

*2. Wind carries the water vapor over land until it begins to cool. The cooled water falls to Earth as rain or snow.*

*3. The rain and melted snow collect in rivers. The rivers carry the water back to the ocean.*

*1. The sun heats the surface of the ocean. This causes some of the water to evaporate.*

# Climate

Winds over the Pacific Ocean affect the climate. Winds that blow westward along the **equator** are called the trade winds. They begin in the eastern Pacific and blow at a steady speed. The trade winds carry warm, moist air that creates pleasant weather.

Every few years, the trade winds stop. As the winds shift, warm water spreads east to the normally cool waters of Ecuador and Peru. The change in water temperature kills ocean animals and causes floods and **droughts**. This event is called El Niño.

Monsoons also affect the west Pacific's climate. In the winter, these winds blow from the land toward the ocean. This creates cold, dry weather. In the summer, the winds shift. They blow from the ocean toward the land. This brings heavy rains.

Storms called tropical cyclones occur in the Pacific. They are called typhoons in the western Pacific and hurricanes in the eastern Pacific. They form over warm ocean water. Some of these storms reach land, bringing high winds and heavy rains.

*A monsoon storm brings heavy rains to a farm in Queensland, Australia.*

# Plants

Two main types of plants grow in the Pacific Ocean. One type grows on the ocean floor. The other type floats on the water's surface.

Phytoplankton are plants that float on the Pacific's surface. These tiny plants are too small to see without a microscope. Though they are small, phytoplankton are important. They form the base of the ocean's **food chain**.

Sea grasses also grow in the Pacific Ocean. Southeast Asia's coast contains one of the world's richest sea grass areas. Sea grass roots stabilize the sand they grow in. They also provide food, shelter, and breeding areas for many ocean animals.

A type of seaweed called kelp grows in the Pacific, too. Kelp attaches to rocks along the coasts of North and South America. Kelp has large, broad leaves. It can grow to be 100 feet (30 m) tall! Kelp forests shelter fish, snails, crabs, starfish, and other animals.

*Fish swim through a kelp forest.*

# Animals

The Pacific Ocean contains many animal species. Zooplankton are a group of animals that are weak swimmers. For this reason, zooplankton drift with the ocean's currents. Pacific zooplankton include jellyfish, krill, and shrimp.

Nekton make up the group of animals that can swim freely in the ocean. Nekton include a wide variety of species, such as fish, sharks, seals, dolphins, octopuses, snakes, and whales.

Benthos are the group of animals that spend their lives on the ocean floor. These animals include starfish, oysters, snails, lobsters, and worms.

The Pacific Ocean is also home to coral. Coral are small animals that live in colonies. When they die, coral leave behind hard skeletons. Over many years, the skeletons form coral **reefs** such as the Great Barrier Reef. It extends 1,250 miles (2,012 km) along Australia's northeast coast.

*The Great Barrier Reef*

# Natives & Explorers

The Pacific Ocean has more than 10,000 islands. People from Southeast Asia **migrated** to many of these islands thousands of years ago. They were the first known settlers of this region. One such group of settlers is the Maori.

The Maori settled on the island of New Zealand. They obtained food, such as fish and seaweed, from the Pacific. They traveled the Pacific in canoes made of hollowed tree trunks. Today, the Maori are still an important part of New Zealand's **culture**.

Though native peoples had known of the Pacific for years, Europeans first discovered it in 1513. That year, a Spaniard named Vasco Núñez de Balboa discovered the Pacific Ocean while exploring Panama.

In 1520, Portuguese explorer Ferdinand Magellan led the first known crossing of the Pacific. In the late 1700s, British explorer James Cook made accurate maps of the Pacific. He also discovered many of its islands, including Hawaii.

The Waka Huia Maori Culture Group performs
at a local celebration.  Groups such as this
preserve the Maori culture for the future.

# Today's Pacific

The Pacific Ocean provides people with many natural resources. Fish caught in the Pacific are a major food source. Valuable oil and gas fields lie under the ocean floor. Minerals, such as salt, are taken from the Pacific's waters. And ships travel on the Pacific to transport goods and raw materials.

These activities, however, have damaged the Pacific. For example, in 1989, a ship called the *Exxon Valdez* crashed into a **reef** near Alaska. The crash damaged the ship, which spilled 11 million gallons (42 million liters) of oil into the Pacific. The oil spill killed thousands of birds, otters, seals, whales, and fish.

In addition, polluted rivers enter the Pacific. This hurts the ocean and its wildlife. **Overfishing** has reduced the population of many kinds of fish. And many nations dump waste into the Pacific. For these reasons, many groups are working to preserve the Pacific Ocean for the future.

*The Pacific Coast, near California*

# Glossary

**culture** - the customs, arts, and tools of a nation or people at a certain time.

**dense** - having a large amount of matter in a given volume.

**dissolve** - to break down and spread evenly throughout a liquid.

**drought** - a long period of dry weather.

**equator** - an imaginary circle around the middle of Earth.

**food chain** - an arrangement of plants and animals in a community. Each plant or animal feeds on other plants or animals in a certain order. For example, phytoplankton are eaten by small fish, small fish are eaten by large fish, and large fish are eaten by humans.

**migrate** - to move from one place to settle in another.

**molten** - melted by heat.

**overfish** - to catch so many fish that the number of fish in a given body of water is greatly reduced.

**reef** - a chain of rocks or coral, or a ridge of sand, near the water's surface.

**sea** - a body of water that is smaller than an ocean and is almost completely surrounded by land.

**sea level** - the average height of all the oceans. It is often used to measure height or depth, with sea level as zero feet.

**tropics of Cancer and Capricorn** - two imaginary lines on Earth just north and south of the equator. The area between the tropics of Cancer and Capricorn marks the position farthest north and south where the sun shines directly overhead at noon.

# How Do You Say That?

**cyclone** - SI-klohne
**El Niño** - ehl NEE-nyo
**Macquarie** - muh-KWAR-ee
**Maori** - MOUR-ee
**Mariana** - mahr-ee-AH-nuh
**Pangaea** - pan-JEE-uh
**Panthalassa** - pan-THA-luh-suh
**phytoplankton** - fi-toh-PLANGK-tuhn
**tsunami** - suh-NAH-mee
**typhoon** - ti-FOON
**Vasco Núñez de Balboa** - VAS-ko NOO-nyez day bal-BO-uh
**zooplankton** - zoh-uh-PLANGK-tuhn

# Web Sites

Would you like to learn more about the Pacific Ocean?  Please visit
**www.abdopub.com** to find up-to-date Web site links about the Pacific
Ocean and its creatures.  These links are routinely monitored and
updated to provide the most current information available.

# Index